ROYAL SCOTTISH STATUTES

ROYAL SCOTTISH STATUTES

ALEXANDER II KING OF SCOTS

Copyright 2025 by Dalcassian Press

All rights reserved. No part of this book may be reproduced in any manner whatsoever without written permission except in the case of brief quotations embodied in critical articles and reviews.

No part of this publication may be reproduced, distributed, or transmitted in any form or by any means, including photocopying, recording, or other electronic or mechanical methods, without the prior written permission of the publisher, except in the case of brief quotations embodied in critical reviews and certain other non-commercial uses permitted by copyright law. For permission request, write to Dalcassian Press at admin@thescriptoriumproject.com

Translator: Curtin, D.P. (1985-)

ISBN: 979-8-3484-6591-9 (Paperback)
ISBN: 979-8-3484-6590-2 (eBook)
Library of Congress Control Number:

Printed by Ingram Content Group, 1 Ingram Blvd, La Vergne, Tennessee
First Printing 2025, Dalcassian Press, Wilmington, DE

This work is part of a series produced in association with the Scriptorium Project and its community of scholars and translators.
Please visit our website at: www.thescriptoriumproject.com

STATES OF KING ALEXANDER II, SON OF WILLIAM

CHAPTER I: ON AGRICULTURE.

1. In the year of grace one thousand two hundred and fourteen. At Scone, Alexander by the grace of God King of Scots, in a common council of the Earls held for the benefit of the country, decreed that all peasants in the same places and villages where they were in the past year, should exercise agriculture this year; and that they should not delay their progress, but should begin to plow and sow their lands with all diligence fifteen days before the Purification of the Blessed Virgin Mary.

2. Furthermore, the King and the Princes established that farmers who have more than four cows should seek sustenance for themselves and their families; they should take and cultivate lands under their lords.

3. However, all those who have less than four cows, although they cannot plow, may still dig the earth with their hands and feet to acquire for themselves and sustain their lives as much as they are able.

4. If they have oxen, those who cultivate the land by plowing and sowing should sell them.

5. Counts and Barons in whose lands such people reside, unwilling to do this in their County, shall purchase eight cows for the King.

6. If anyone holding from the King neglects to do this, he shall give to the King, for the offense, eight cows. If he holds from a Count, he shall give only to the Count.

7. If he is a servant, let his Lord take at this time one cow as a fine, and a sheep. And henceforth, let him compel him to do what he was unwilling to do voluntarily.

8. Therefore, it is very necessary to take care that what is said in parables does not happen to them: Because of the cold, the lazy man did not want to plow in winter, he will beg in summer, and he will not be given to. But rather, according to the Apostle's opinion, let them work with their hands doing what is good; that they may have something to give to those in need.

CHAPTER II: ON THE INDICTMENTS TO BE DECEIVED AND ON PUNISHING MALEFACTORS

1. King Alexander, illustrious King of Scots, establishes, by the counsel and consent of the Venerable Fathers, Bishops, Abbots, Counts, Barons, and good men of his Kingdom; that his Justiciar of Lothian shall diligently and privately make an inquiry into the malefactors of the land and their receivers; through the oaths of three good and faithful men, along with the oath of the Seneschal, from each village, of each Sheriffdom within his Bailiwick, except in Galloway, which has its own special laws.

2. And if he finds anyone, through the said legally established inquiry, let him be hastily attached by the servants of the Lord King, with the help of the men of the Lord of the village, and let them be brought safely to a certain day and place before the Justiciar; through faithful neighborhood let them be transferred.

3. Nevertheless, if any of them is convicted of murder, robbery, or similar felonies pertaining to the crown of the Lord King, all their goods shall remain with the Lord King without any contradiction...

4. If, however, someone is convicted of theft, homicide, or similar felonies pertaining to theft or homicide; the goods they have in the lands of the Lords shall remain those same goods without any contradiction.

5. The Lord King also decreed that no one shall henceforth be attached by the servants of the Lord King, except by the aforementioned inquiry if they are indicted for felony.

6. All convicted of theft or homicide shall be handed over to the Justiciar, Barons, or their Bailiffs to administer justice upon them in their free Baronies, without any redemption or remedy, unless the grace of the Lord King intervenes.

7. Likewise, if any Knight has been indicted for his wrongdoing by a faithful neighbor of Knights or free tenants through the aforementioned inquiry, he shall be hereditary transferred.

8. Furthermore, Attachors, on account of their attachments, shall carry nothing from the goods of the attached person: Nor shall they consume anything from them. But the Lord of the village or his Seneschal shall reasonably sustain them for one day and night from the goods of the attached person.

CHAPTER III: ASSESSMENT OF LIFE, MEMBER, OR LAND MUST BE MADE BY FREE TENANTS

Moreover, the Lord King Alexander decreed at Strivelin, in the presence of his Magnates, both ecclesiastical men and others: That henceforth, no oath shall be taken regarding the loss of life, or the limbs of a man, or land, except by faithful men and by good free tenants by Charters.

CHAPTER IV: WHO CAN BE PARDONED

1. The King decreed by the counsel and assent of the whole community of his subjects that no Bishop, Abbot, or Cleric of the kingdom of Scotland, someone will reclaim him as his man, nor will he seek a pledge from anyone who has been caught in any crime, unless the same person has been accused, has been his liege man, or is native, or residing in his land, or of his household.

2. And if he can be recognized by lawful men of the country; that the wrongdoer is not a liege man, or native, or residing in the land, or of the household of the reclaimant, but that the same reclaimant has wished to reclaim the accused, for some mercenary cause, as the Magnates have been accustomed to do, taking from the wrongdoer wax, pepper, cumin, or any other commodity) the wealthy reclaimant shall be in the mercy of the Lord King.

CHAPTER V: OF THEFT COMMITTED BY RELIGIOUS MEN AND OTHERS WHO ARE NOT BOUND TO FIGHT.

1. Therefore, the Lord King has established that if anything has been secretly stolen from religious men, clerics, widows, prebendaries, or such as cannot fight, nor should: the complainants shall come to the lord of the fee, or his bailiff: and he himself, the bailiff, or his appointed sheriff, shall, without delay, according to the proportion of three baronies, diligently and faithfully inquire by lawful men of the vicinity, who that wrongdoer was.

2. And if according to that proportion the wrongdoer is found or convicted, let just judgment be rendered.

3. And if he has fled, nonetheless, the religious men, widows, and other complainants shall have restored what was taken from them from the goods of the wrongdoer, and their remaining belongings shall belong to the Lord King; or to whom they are rightfully owed.

4. If, however, in the domains or thanages of the Lord King, that wrongdoer has been; the sheriff shall act without delay as stated above.

CHAPTER VI: DUTIES TO THE CHURCH

1. Regarding those who flee to the Church from robbers and thieves, we decree that if any of them repents, confesses there that he has gravely sinned, and seeks peace for the love of God for his salvation, he shall have peace in this way, namely, that he shall neither lose his life nor his limbs; but whatever he has unjustly taken from someone else, he shall restore to him, and according to the law of the father, he shall make amends to the Lord King.

2. And upon the text of the Gospel, he shall swear that from now on he will never commit robbery or theft.

3. And if he cannot pay what is owed to the Lord King, he shall fulfill the other aforementioned conditions; and in that peace, he shall go abroad until he is reconciled with the Lord King.

4. However, if anyone among them, fleeing to the Church, wishes to show himself innocent, saying that he feared a rash power, so that he may be allowed to purify himself according to the law, let him go in peace to the Court of the Lord King, and there, from whom he has been accused, let him provide sureties and pledges according to the custom of the land. And if there he purifies himself according to the law of the land, let him remain in peace.

5. But if anyone is justly and legally convicted of a crime brought against him, let him submit to the judgment that such a defendant deserves, according to the law of the land and the kingdom.

6. And if anyone among them flees to the Church, confessing that he is innocent, but because of poverty cannot find sureties or pledges in any place where it seems safe and suitable to the Lord King or the Bishop, let him purify himself according to judgment; hence if he is found clean, let him remain in peace. And if he is found unclean, let him receive the sentence that he deserves.

7. Moreover, murderers or betrayers of their lords, and those who are accused of murder or treachery or committed theft; they shall be lawfully accused of this. And if they have been falsely accused in the aforementioned ways, and have fled to the Church; the prescribed law shall be observed concerning them.

CHAPTER VII: ON FALSE ACCUSATION OF THEFT, AND ROBBERY, AND THE ABROGATION OF PURIFICATION.

1. If anyone falsely accuses someone of theft, or robbery; and the defendant wishes to defend himself based on the proportion of neighbors; and if the neighbors themselves have purified him, he shall be free. And he who appeals shall remain in the mercy of the Lord King.

2. But if he is not purified, let just judgment be made concerning him.

3. And henceforth, let there be no judgment by water, or iron; as was customary in ancient times.

CHAPTER VIII: ON UNJUST RULINGS.

1. If anyone complains to the Lord King, or Justiciar, that his Lord or someone else has unjustly and without judgment disseized him of something, of which he was seized and vested, and has found pledges

for pursuing his claim, the Justiciar, or sheriff shall make recognition by the good men of the country, if the complainant has spoken the truth or made a just complaint, by the command of the King or the Justiciar.

2. And if it is thus recognized and proven: the Justiciar, or Vice-comes, shall proceed to restore the seized thing, concerning which there was a dispute. And the disseisor shall be in the mercy of the Lord King.

3. And if a Knight, or another, has made the said disseisin, he shall remain in the mercy of the Lord King.

4. And those goods, or land, shall be immediately restored to the present Court, with damages or arrears, to the disseisee.

5. If, however, it is recognized that the complainant made an unjust complaint: he shall be in the mercy of the Lord King, and shall pay a fine of ten pounds.

CHAPTER IX: WOMEN PETITIONING FOR A THIRD PART, OR DOTAL PORTION.

When a long controversy has arisen in the Court of the Lord King between E., the wife of the late B., on one side petitioning for a third part of the land of D. with its appurtenances, in the name of a third part, justly, and according to the Assize of the third part: of the lands which belonged to B., her husband, with its appurtenances: And H., the son of the Count of S., on the other side, having the custody of the lands that belonged to the said B. And conversely, asserting that he should not be entitled to any part in the said land of B. according to the Assize of the land: because the mother of B. held the said land in dotal portion, after the death of the said B., her son; nor did the widow woman become accustomed, according to the custom of the kingdom, to obtain a third of such land. Finally, the Lord King, concerning this, established a certain law to be upheld in his kingdom, that any widow, having the right to claim her dowry after the death of her husband, shall henceforth be entitled to claim a third part of this, as well as the entirety of the remainder. And many nobles were present.

CHAPTER X: OF THOSE WHO REFUSE TO PURSUE IN COURT

1. If anyone has been wronged by someone in any complaint, of injury, and not by reason: And finds pledges for pursuing, and does not wish to pursue, he falls into the mercy of the Lord King.

2. Likewise, if anyone has been convicted of seeking judgment, he shall fall into the mercy of the Lord King.

3. Likewise, if he has no pledges for pursuing, he shall be in mercy.

4. And if he refuses to pursue after having taken an oath, he shall be captured and detained in prison for his offense.

5. And if anyone has been wronged by someone in any complaint; such as concerning life and limbs; and has no pledges for pursuing, he shall be detained in reasonable and secure prison until he has received judgment.

CHAPTER XI: PENALTY FOR THOSE CONVICTED IN DUEL.

If anyone has been wronged in any complaint pertaining to the crown of the Lord King, from which a duel may arise, he shall fall into calumny in battle: his pledges shall respond to the Lord King, with nine cows and one colpindach, and shall satisfy the calumniator for his calumny, which pertains to his evasion.

CHAPTER XII: STOLEN PROPERTY MUST BE BROUGHT TO THE DESIGNED PLACES.

The King has decreed regarding stolen property, that in whichever province property is found to be stolen and claimed, it shall be taken to a place in any county: where King David decreed that claimed property should be returned.

CHAPTER XIII: A THIEF WITHOUT A LORD OR PLEDGE.

The Lord King has decreed that if someone is accused of theft in one province or two, and is found without any Lord who is unwilling to provide a pledge for him, he shall be treated as a proven thief.

CHAPTER XIV: THE VICEROY MUST BE PRESENT AT THE COURTS OF BISHOPS, ABBOTS, COUNTS AND OTHERS.

1. It is decreed that neither Bishops, nor Abbots, nor Counts, nor any freeholders shall hold their Courts unless the King's Viceroy or the servants of the Viceroy are present there, or summoned to be present, to see if the Court is conducted properly.

2. And in all their Courts, four pleas shall be reserved for the Court of the Lord King, which pertain to the crown, namely, concerning the abduction of a woman, arson, murder, and robbery, which is called plunder.

3. And if the Viceroy, when summoned, does not come to the Court of the Baron, nor sends anyone from the King's servants, it shall be lawful for the Baron to hold his Court legally, without the King's forfeit.

4. Regarding other complaints, each of the freeholders who have a Court shall hold it for whatever happens there, saving the mercy of the Lord King.

CHAPTER XV: FOR THE RELIEF OF THE EXCLUDED FROM THE KING'S ARMY.

1. A record made before Lord King Alexander, at the great assembly of Lent, after the King had been in the army at Inverness against Donald son of Nigell of the Isles of those who were absent from the army. That the King should have the exemption of the Earl, if any of them have remained from the army, but it was not discussed there, how much it should be.

2. Moreover, concerning all others who have remained from the army, namely, the lesser bishops, abbots, barons, knights, thanes, who hold from the King, only the King should have the exemption. Namely, from the thane six cows and one heifer. From the oxen fifteen sheep, or six shillings, but the King will not have more than half of this, and the thane or knight the other half. From the rustic one cow and one sheep, and these similarly should be divided between the King and the thane or knight.

3. But if by the license of the thane or knight, they have remained from the King's army, the King alone will have the exemption.

4. However, no earl or servants of the earl should come to the land of anyone holding from the King to demand this exemption, except the Earl of Fife, to demand his rights.

5. Concerning the calves, where the King and the Earl divide, the King and the Earl shall have one half of the exemption from the army, and the Thane the other half.

6. But where the thane himself is in the exemption, the exemption shall be divided between the King and the Earl.

CHAPTER XVI: SUNDRY LAWS.

1. This is the decree of King Alexander, made at Perth, on Thursday, before the feast of Margaret, by the earls, barons, and judges of Scotland, that the stream of water or the middle of the water, namely the stream, shall be free for use everywhere to such an extent that one pig, three years old, well-fed, can turn itself within the pigsty: so that neither the snout of the pig nor the tail approaches the hedge or the bank.

2. And the water should be free: so that no one may fish there from the Sabbath day, after vespers, until the Monday after the rising of the sun.

CHAPTER XVII: ON THE JUDGMENT OF GILASCOPE

On the Sunday next after the feast of Saint Dionysius, in the chapter of the Abbot of the Holy Cross; concerning Gilascope Mak-Scolane, it was judged by all judges both of Scotland and Galloway, that the aforementioned Gilascope had not brought pledges on the appointed day, for which he was to give pledges, on the appointed day and place, he himself was the pledger. Therefore, he must give pledges to the King, so that the King may be at peace. And if he cannot give pledges at the King's will, he himself shall remain in pledge; until he has given the promised pledges. And furthermore, if he does otherwise: in the grave mercy of the Lord King, he shall remain.

CHAPTER XVIII: ON MANELET

1. If your farmer places a manelet on the land of the King, or of a Baron: and does not wish to remove and cleanse it, he must be punished, just like a seducer, who leads an army into the land of the King or Baron.

2. Likewise, if your tenant has a manelet on your land, for any plant, he shall give you, or to any other lord of his, a sheep, for his wrongdoing. And nonetheless, he shall cleanse the land of the manelet.

CHAPTER XIX: ON FALSE CHARTER

1. Whoever is convicted of having made a false charter, his hand shall be cut off.

2. Not only of the one who made the falsity; but also of anyone who was knowingly present.

CHAPTER XX: PRIVILEGE OF THE ELEEMOSYNARY LAND.

1. Furthermore, King Alexander prohibits that any minister of the King shall take anything from the Eleemosynary lands, nor from his men, for the work of the Lord King.

2. Unless that thing cannot be found on the land of the Lord King, or in the Baronies.

3. And in that case, that thing shall be taken by the view of the Sergeants of the Lord of that Eleemosynary land.

CHAPTER XXI: CONCERNING RECEIVERS OF THEFT.

Whoever knowingly receives stolen goods shall be held accountable.

CHAPTER XXII: CONCERNING THE RESTITUTION OF DOWRY.

1. A widow, after the death of her husband, shall immediately and without any difficulty have her marriage portion and her inheritance.

2. Nor shall she give anything for her dowry, her marriage portion, or her inheritance, other than the inheritance that her husband and she held on the day of her husband's death.

3. And she shall remain in the capital without her husband for forty days after the death of her husband. After those days, her dowry shall be assigned to her; unless it has already been assigned to her, or unless that house has been a castle.

4. And if she has withdrawn from the castle, she shall be immediately provided with a suitable house in which she can reside honorably, until her dowry is assigned to her, as previously stated, and she shall have reasonable sustenance from the common fund in the meantime.

5. However, let a third part of the entire dowry be assigned to her, which was hers in her lifetime, unless it has been endowed to the Church.

CHAPTER XXIII: A WIDOW IS NOT COMPELLED TO REMARRY, BUT SHE MUST HAVE THE CONSENT OF HER DECEASED HUSBAND TO MARRY.

No widow shall be compelled to marry, as long as she wishes not to marry herself, without our consent, if she has held from us, without the consent of her husband, if she holds from another than us.

CHAPTER XXIV: THE PAYMENT OF DEBTS, AND THE SALE OF DEBTOR'S LANDS.

1. If the debtor, or his inhabitants, have movable goods, they must first be distrained to pay the creditor.

2. And if they have no movable goods to be distrained, the Vicecomes and ministers of the King shall warn the debtor, before the raising of the Court; that in the absence of movables, he is obliged to sell the debtor's lands and possessions, within fifteen days, to satisfy the creditor.

3. But if the debtor himself does not do so within fifteen days, the Vicecomes and ministers of the King shall sell those lands and possessions of the debtor; according to the custom of the kingdom; until the creditor is satisfied, of the principal sum, with damages, expenses, and interest.

4. And the Vicecomes shall enfeoff the purchaser, by the Charter of the King, if they are held from the Regent.

5. And if they are held from a Baron, and he wishes to buy them, he is deemed to have the right.

6. And if another wishes to have them for the price of the King, the Vicecomes shall enfeoff the purchaser, in the manner the debtor held them, with his Birebs, and all appurtenances.

7. However, the Baron shall receive the purchaser, at the command of the Vicecomes, and shall give the original seisin of the debtor, without obstruction, or any kind of question.

CHAPTER XXV: WRECKS OF THE SEA.

1. If any ship, vessel, or other craft has been wrecked, and a man, dog, or living mouse is found, and exits, the goods from that wreck shall not be adjudicated for the benefit of the sea: But they shall be safeguarded with all the goods, by the authority of the Vice-Count, the Coronator, or the Royal Bailiff, and it shall be decided in their hands in the town where those things are found. So that if anyone claims those goods, and can prove that they are his own, or belong to his lord, or that they were lost in his custody; they shall be returned to him within that year and day without delay. And if not, they shall remain with the King: they shall be taken by the Vice-Count, the Coronator, or the Bailiff; and they shall be delivered to those of the town, who shall respond to this before the justice, regarding the matter concerning the King.

2. And where the wreck belongs to someone other than the Lord King; they shall have it in the same manner.

3. And whoever does otherwise and is convicted of this shall be attainted: he shall be placed in prison, and there shall be kept and redeemed according to the royal will.

This work was produced in association with:

www.ingramcontent.com/pod-product-compliance
Lightning Source LLC
LaVergne TN
LVHW061050070526
838201LV00074B/5246